THE POETRY OF SHROPSHIRE

✦

Perton Library
24hr Renewal Line
Tel: 0345 330 0740

Borrowed Items 06/03/2019 12:

XXXXXXXXXX6712

Indicates ite   today

hank you for using Self Serve

hank you for visiting Your Library

ww.staffordshire.gov.uk/libraries

THE POETRY OF SHROPSHIRE

✦

Edited by
Simon Fletcher & Jeff Phelps

OFFA'S PRESS
2013

First published 2013 by Offa's Press
Ferndale, Pant, Oswestry, Shropshire, SY10 9QD
Reprinted in 2014

ISBN 978-0-9565518-5-6

Typeset in Baskerville Old Face

Designed by Marie Campbell

Printed by Graphics and Print, Hortonwood, Telford

Contents

Mistletoe, near Richards Castle

In the month of the Green Man,
the soft road cleaves the hills,
and in the rain the pedlar
walks his miles between farms,
in a dream of bare hedges
knotted with ribbons.

He says,
what's without soil, but touching darkness?
He says,
what's without flight, but airborne?
He says,
what's without water, but still green-mouthed?
He says:
without kisses, my bitter one, out
go the fires.

He cuts it and binds it in ribbons and climbs
this footprinted hill, in his time still
all threats and ramparts. Shakes off
its round horizon, its ashes,
carries the old ways over
the thresholds.

Jean Atkin

Autumn

Spare me the Shropshire autumn.
If I knew how, I'd leave before September has the time
To touch the trees – return when they are bare.
It makes me sad, the scent of autumn in the air.

Even the gardens wear more mauve and purple now,
The shades of mourning, as the summer fades.

I find too wide, the scope for sadness here,
So many woods; and Wenlock Edge
Has broken better hearts than mine.
This is the territory of tears:
I'd rather take off for the town, for coward that I am
I shrink from facing autumn fears.

The trees will wear again
In spring, the green of youth;

But autumn knows the melancholy truth:
I shall be older then.

Mollie Bolt

The Stiperstones

I sit in the Devil's Chair,
tumble a lump of seabed in my hands.
Pebbledashed and flecked with peat,
it looks like a nugget from a 1960s house,
not a five-hundred-million-year-old find.
Heavy
like the clouds sitting on the circular horizon,

a giant bowl
filled with overlapping hills
like whipped cake mixture.
This one is meringue,
quartzite like sugar.
Tufts of bilberry bush offer an accompaniment.

Two wrens abrasively scold,
disappointed by this peak.
Not high enough to merit the full kit -
yet groups with boots,
cags,
sticks,
stand at the base of my outcrop.

I want to sleep on these bedding planes,
to be found 'inspired or insane'.
But nearby, Caer Caradoc lies like a dinosaur that is only resting,
ravens cronk overhead,
and I am convinced of the smell of brimstone.

Rosamund Brown

Standard Class

'If I had the quaint Muse of Sir Philip Sidney to assist me,
I would write a *Sonnet to the Road between Wem and
Shrewsbury,* and immortalise every step of it'
– William Hazlitt, *My First Acquaintance with Poets*

I have no Coleridge for company
and road is replaced by a crusty seat,
heater, flip-down table and the raw stench
of weed. Sock-tucked-tracksuit wearers, harvest
from Saxon Fields estate, sit by the sign:
Drugproof Your Kids. Large yellow squares of rape
flash. Indecently bright. Punctuated
by cherry trees in blossom, not quite white.
We pass through Yorton (request stop only).
The line that slipped off Beeching's block creeps round

the back of town; Travelodge, BT Fleet;
cables like worms by the wayside, escaped
from Battlefield and its dark, slimy things.
Shrewsbury evolves. The tannoy gruffly sings.

Rosamund Brown

From **The River**

Down there in the valley
The Severn runs wide and slow
And that's where I caught a seven-pound trout
On a morning with mist smoking above the surface
And the blossom drifting down off the trees.
It was running up from the estuary
Making for the pool where it was born
When it latched itself onto my bait.
And I can feel it now, the whump and drag
On my arms, the slamming, cast-iron weight
Jolt through my shoulder, nearly pulling me in –
The writhing, thrashing, banging life of it
Like reeling in the river itself
Ripping it up out of its rootbed
From source to sea, the whole country
With my hook in its lip
Like a great English dragon
Shedding scales and light,
A scattering of rainbows.

David Calcutt

Hopton Castle

Rowan and elder
make a wild garden
here, grapple for light
at the austere

arches; ashsaplings
crane, crack stone
up the tiny crumbled stair.

This was a minor garrison
in empty hills, leaf-
crepitating:-
no prince, no belle dame.

But there was a siege
once, a betrayal,
a slaughter:
the moat water
holds they say old bones.

Under the weeping willows
the cattle drink
breast-metal, trothless irons.

Vuyelwa Carlin

Coalport Girls

Who like you
could magic up, plate after plate,
the fuzz of peach, the frosty glow of grapes?
Or put a tear drop on the peony's cheek
fresh as your own
wet from the fields of Shropshire or East Wales?
Or paint to order a bouquet of birds,
the colour not yet faded from their necks?
Lips blue with cobalt and with cold,
brush hairs spit-licked to a point,
could gild a rim, so trimly roundelled
no Lady might detect its true beginnings,
then replicate her new escutcheon
on cup and saucer, creamer, bonbon dish…
I have seen photographs in faded sepia –
your beauty bundled up in man-sized aprons,
seated at trestles, piecework piled high
behind, in front, like tower blocks;
or on a charabanc outing to Llangollen,
bolt upright in your Sunday collars,
hands tight-gripped against unbusyness,
and wondered at the tiredness of your smiles.
But not as pale as on that black-edged day
a row of lodgings, undermined,
spilled casually downhill towards the Severn.
When they dug you out, your upturned faces
and clay filled mouths, wide open gazes
once glazed the colours of a summer morning,
now whitish grey –
dull as the slipware before it is ghost fired.

Keith Chandler

Calling on Ivy

At Lilleshall they said
she's no longer here.
She's moved.
She didn't like
the wind whistling in the trees.
The house was damp,
the cobwebs grew.
She's down at Donnington by now.

At Donnington they said
she's no longer here.
She's moved.
She didn't like the way
the sun made shadows in the hall.
The back door creaked.
The mice were rude.
She's down at Muxton now.

At Muxton they said
she left last week.
She didn't like
the muddy fields,
the dog next door,
the farmer's horse.
She's down at Telford now.

At Telford
they said she's left for good.
Not sure where she's gone
she changed her mind so much.
St Peter's, Christ the King,
St Leonard's, St George's or Holy Trinity.
God knows where Ivy's gone.

Marion Cockin

The Peat Cutters

They know the calendar by the mosses' hues:
in winter, the slow erasure of colour
frost-blanched to tones of ash and oat
where the kestrel keeps faith with the field mouse,
the sedge shivers in a raking wind,
low moan of advancing snow.
White-out. The hummocks of the bog
are a sea of frozen breakers.

At melt-time the peat-cutters return;
their sabots squelch, their spades slit,
slick through. They lifted embedded stones
where water seeps, the level rising,
reversing desiccation. New cuttings rough-hewn –
each one at night a trough of stars.

*

Some evenings, stumbling home in mist
their shapes emerge; others blow whistles
when dark falls on fog, the bog sucks.
Say bog, think of bodies – soil's store
in an acid hold preserving –
perhaps, too, the bones of mammoths.
Peat-cutters fear they'll slice through flesh.

One's convinced he's seen Judge Jeffreys,
heard his haunting horn, horses' hammer,
shriek of fox, like mandrakes torn.
Baron of Wem, his estate 'The Law',
'Bloodfingers' Jeffreys dealt in death,
gibbets gorged with Sedgemoor rebels
trapped like flies in the sundew.

*

Below zero: the earth again iced-locked –
cuttings grow new skin; twigs balance upright.
Peat-workers stare at sculpted ground, white roots
tapping down ten thousand years. These black zones
could be an entrance to the Underworld
where Charon waits on the bog-bordered Styx.

They stack their turves, feed some to the shredder,
mindful of fingers, arms, how old Joe died.
Yet Spring's sneaking in like a svelte grass-snake,
the sphagnum's now greening, like birds linking song.
Soon, orchid, rosemary, bog asphodel
will follow emerald, their colour of hope.

From **The Women of Whixall**

Agnes Morris – Making Whixall Wreaths
Custom dating back to 1915

'The holly and the ivy
When they are both full grown…'
Clipped from the bough each year
from the same trees in Shropshire's russet crown,
the prickly harvest falls reluctantly
into our hands. Dark green shine
for Christmas wreaths, softened by sphagnum,
top moss dried, arranged on frames.
With fingers increasingly tender
we weave in kitchens in December.

Gladys Mary Coles

Wings

Moreton Corbett, near RAF Shawbury

A thunderous roar of engines fills the sky
As sleek winged jet planes soar into the blue
And rotored helicopters whirling by
Make airborne, for a while, their human crew.
A skylark soars, regardless of the noise,
Effortlessly rising on small wings
Over its nest, well hidden in the grass,
And in its soaring, joyfully it sings.
Pert lapwing wheel in wild erratic flight,
While from the rook-filled wood the cuckoo calls;
And jackdaws, busy building nests, fly out
And in these ruined crumbled walls.
A bumble bee with pollen laden sacs
All self-absorbed, investigating flowers,
Flies, drunk with nectar, round the clover patch,
Well occupied in daylight's busy hours.
Small ladybirds, mosquitoes, butterflies –
The world is filled with gauzy flutt'ring wings:
And over all, the screaming powerful jet,
Man's contribution to the scheme of things.

Janet Collins

I Walk Around Ellesmere

I walk around Ellesmere
    As if one foot put in front of another

        Captures the measure of water

    Or the dimensions of a ghost
Contracted to water surrounded by land

How long do I walk before I realise
    That my footprints erase themselves,

        That I am in the middle of the mere

    Strolling on water and not alone
But in a crowd of ghost walkers?

This is a dream, I tell myself,
    Only a dream, when I wake

        My feet will be on firm ground and dry.

    But I do not wake, I keep walking
Out to the middle of the mere

Where I am welcomed as a long lost
    Friend home at last to water and air,

        To midnight, and me out in the open

    At a festival of airy presences
All with a date and each in the head

Of the living who sleep and give over
    Themselves to these ghosts and this

        Ghost-coloured water in midnight walks

    That feed the mere with stories
And each story as heavy as water, and as cold.

Fred D'Aguiar

Housman & Me

Splayed like winter twigs –
my mother's calligraphics
were tacked onto the wall.

I repeated the lines like ghosts
replaying a moment –
chewed on the words,

while the kids at school
had badges, hairbands, pencil cases,
emblazoned with their names.

A slither in a book,
found one lifeless afternoon –
its letters stars in my eyes.

To think!
That *I* was 'the loveliest of trees',
charming in my Easter bloom.

'To see the cherry hung with snow',
reminded me of how I was named –
for all seasons of life.

Blossom in my brain,
my mother sat and scribed the verse
for my bedroom wall.

Housman's cherry tree,
'About the woodland' and on the page,
captivated him and me.

Cherry Doyle

Dene House, Broseley, Revisited

Past the pub,
the war memorial,
the lane is just the same.
I pull up in a haze
of cow parsley, remember the trick
of opening the white gate.
The trees have grown
in the side garden
where I read novels in the morning.
Roses cascade on the rustic arch.
Wellington boots, still, in the porch.

It is evening, and the sun sets
over the pool, insects frantic in the golden haze.
The tapestries remain on the sitting room wall.
Upstairs, I revisit
the wide landing, the photograph of
the mysterious girl on a horse.
The bedrooms seem just the same:
the one where my aunt saw a ghost,
mine where I watched the sun rise
over the trees. Later I go to your yoga den –
a fading smell of new timber.

Night.
The fabulous stars
and owls still call
from the black wood.
The moon rises.

Susan Fearn

Archivist

There have always been men like this,
silent in libraries, deep in old files.

You know them, dogged researchers,
diligently tracking trails of letters;

women who sit over tea and disinter
the scandals and histories of their neighbours,

who call a house Cotton's, though he's long been dead,
slip back decades into maiden names,

know what was there before the council houses,
rehearse with pleasure rows of vanished shops.

Let's salute the fingerers of the past,
noting changes from sepia photographs;

compilers of lists; website nerds
endlessly checking Mormon census cards;

fingers winding microfiche on winter afternoons
in ill-lit basements. All of whom

would hardly notice Gough if he slid in,
took his surcoat off, his wig, and nodded,

pulled out pedigrees and wrote. Searching like us all
for lines of blood and soil

that link us, make us who we are;
this hand, this name, this house, this ancestor.

Catherine Fisher

Loot

"By God...I stand astonished at my own moderation"
Robert Clive to the House of Commons 1772

For Debjani Chatterjee

So I finally got to visit
Walcot- sounds like I'm novelish
and romantic, *n'est-ce pas*, but no
I'm simply on the trail of Clive.
Known in India and the subcontinent
as a villain, a thief,
(stole most of Bengal, let's face it)
in England as a hero, role
model for dashing, daring types an
eighteenth century Thatcherite.
'Go East, young man, fleece the natives',
some corporate wallah from the
'Honourable Company' told

him. 'After all, kick out the French,
they're only Hindoos, worship cows,
monkeys, elephant-headed gods'.
Outside the ballroom, all soft greens
and golds, decaying genteelly,
I should report, I walk across
the lawn, discover the ha ha.
I imagine Clive, one sunny
afternoon, standing here, with the
loot, wrestled by thugs from thugs, safe,
admiring his view and English
cattle and how, in spite of failing
health, he must have laughed and laughed.

Simon Fletcher

Local History

There's anger in Cross Houses, exhaustion in Pant;
great poetry in Homer, laughter in Fitz.

They're minty in Minton, very hopeful in Hope;
but nervous in Twitchen and house-proud in Broome.

They're ghastly in Astley; there's an inlet in Kinlet;
it's murder in Morda with tip-offs in Hints.

They're hopping in Hopton and speeding in Rushton;
they're gambling in Betton and sinking in Moston.

Very squat in Quatt, they're bitter in Bitterley;
dry-eyed in Dryton but embarrassed in Willey.

Never satisfied in More, they grow phlox in Plox;
wrecked around the Wrekin, it's always night in Nox!

Simon Fletcher

Langley Chapel

Up through the short gold stalks
a grey stone submarine
has inched above the ground.

Switch off your phone,
your stored anxieties.
You will not need them here.

Feel free to tread on tiles
whose rich red randomness
obeys no pattern but delight.

Around you, plain white walls.
Ahead, the altar and its benches wait,
aligned in the geometry of prayer.

But there's no rush. Take time.
The solid pews can bear the weight
of patient sinners, doubtful knees.

Over your head the laths and beams
provide a coracle of care. In here
you are protected. Bon voyage.

Paul Francis

Odd Couple

In 1890, Baron Pierre de Coubertin came to visit Dr. William Brookes in Much Wenlock. Both men shared a passion for promoting PE in schools, and in 1896 de Coubertin's modern Olympic Games included features of Wenlock's Olympian Games.

There's more than sixty find their way
through Wenlock's chilly gaslit streets
to the ball above the Corn Exchange.

But two stand out. The honoured guest,
tall, dark, moustachioed, and his host
the venerable Dr. Brookes.

Around them dancers whirl, but they are bound
together by the bug they share,
campaigners arguing for exercise.

Two patient fanatics, hooked on health.
No party chat, no cordon sanitaire
could keep these two apart.

Brookes deals out papers, reams of letters sent,
pleading with Greece to reinvigorate
the old Olympic Games, without reply.

Eighty meets thirty. English, French.
The symptoms of contagion are unclear;
no-one keeps records of a tte-à-tte.

Some thought they glimpsed the ghost of Brookes's son
while others saw a flicker in the gloom,
a torch, maybe, passed on from hand to hand.

Paul Francis

From **Border Songs**

X

Slowly
Thy Kingdom comes

The art and mystery
of casting and moulding
of Iron Potts

after weeks of trial
with the keyhole stopped

Barr Iron
for the Forges
from Pit Coal pigs

after six days and nights
on the bridge of the furnace

Fire Engine Cillinders
Cast Iron rails
an Iron Bridge

all from the refusal
of Friends

plain Friends

to turn cannon
from the Metal of Mars

Roger Garfitt

High Cut

For Jim Elliott

Drawn like blades of earth, the ridges catch light
out of a dull sky. Half-crouched, his arms wide
to the plough handles, a man stalks them as they shear
from the mouldboard. Every other pace
he halts the horses, takes a long spanner
from his back pocket and tightens the outrigging
of press wheel and boats, keels of metal that he draws
on chains, furrow-sharpeners that ride in his wake.

He is the first scribe, perfecting the oldest script.
All alphabets go back to tallies, harvest yields
scratched on clay. The first lines were the lines of increase.
And the shieldwall of books? Breathing spaces we won
when warrior farmers marked out their battleline,
their ridges exact, drawn like blades of earth.

Roger Garfitt

Coalport Morning

Dawn trees
with their long low companionable shadows
they would not be parted from;

it is as if they carry on the breath:
those new earth mornings of candescent light,
spreading their beams across millennia
to reach this place.

Nothing has changed,
nothing escapes the soft flood,
the bright benediction of slant rays
firing up dew, kindling grass
on this next in the chain of first days;

light the frail touch paper
every leaf burns.

Remember that morning
when bird-song dazzled us awake?
And how we lay there then listening
in the hush of the great afterwards silence
that expanded around us;

and then the green, whispering,
calling us,
drawing us out.

Marilyn Gunn

Mole

I know that you are here again,
lurking darkly just beneath the soil
like a migraine waiting to take hold
of my head.

I could become murderous
when I see the rich black-coffee staining
of your fresh mounds, my seedlings
leaned inebriate along your track;

but of course, this is yours, always has been,
while I merely scratch at surfaces. Beneath
are depths of personal darkness:
tunnellings where you power blind,
claws cuffed with velvet,

old freeholder
who feels the narrowing tenure
of my lease.

Marilyn Gunn

Little Heath Green

Steeped in rain, new hawthorn boughs hang heavy.
Each wet leaf droops and drips
and each wet flower tips brim full
and drains,
each drop,
to tease the fox who slips beneath,
doleful, through the sodden gloom
of half-remembered hollow lanes.

Pausing long enough to bare his teeth
and lap the peaty pools
that gather dark and cold along the track he ghosts away
unheard,
alone,
among the rotted hulks of coppiced alder stools
to stop again abrupt,
looking back,
to check that we remain just where we should.
He disappears into the wood,
his silence wrapped in falling rain.

Andrew Harrison (1947-2012)

Ludlow from Whitcliffe

I have given you a silver bracelet;
A brooch of crystal swans; and set
In semi-precious stones, the coloured
Water-birds. How they blaze in sunlight!
Pin there, below, a sapphire kingfisher
Flickering to and fro.

I have given you ear-rings of opal
To wear in all weathers; a necklace
Of emerald beeches to cover the spar
Of your shoulders, and shade the taut skin.
Here the glittering windflower stars the velvet;
Sorrel glows in the secret fold of sleeves.

Take now my boldest gift: a coronet
Of palest gold above your brow,
Delicately braced across the bone,
Holding the fragrant incident of hair -
Bright curling cloud in deep blue air.

Into this haphazard world I send you,
My child, anxious as any parent is,
But confident in these endowments.
The chances of history no-one can foresee,
And time is a stubborn enemy.
Be mild; be strong; be patient. Make me proud.

Peter Holliday

Evening

Lilac blossom crests the window sill
mingling whiteness with the good dark of this room.
A bloom of light hangs delicately in white painted angles.
Bluebells heaped in a pot
still hold their blue against the dark;
I see their green stalks glisten.

Thin as a swan's bone
I wait for the lessons of pain and light.
Grief is a burden, useless.
It must dissolve into the dark.
I see the hills luminous.
There will be a holly tree
the hawthorn with mistletoe
foxgloves springing in thousands.

The hills also will pass away
                will remain
as this lilac light, these bluebells,
the good dark of this room.

Frances Horovitz (1938-1983)

From **A Shropshire Lad**

II

Loveliest of trees, the cherry now
Is hung with bloom along the bough,
And stands about the woodland ride
Wearing white for Eastertide.

Now, of my three-score years and ten,
Twenty will not come again,
And take from seventy springs a score
It only leaves me fifty more.

And since to look at things in bloom
Fifty springs are little room,
About the woodlands I will go
To see the cherry hung with snow.

A.E.Housman

XXXI

On Wenlock Edge the wood's in trouble;
 His forest fleece the Wrekin heaves;
The gale, it plies the saplings double,
 And thick on Severn snows the leaves.

'Twould blow like this through holt and hanger
 When Uricon the city stood:
'Tis the old wind in the old anger,
 But then it threshed another wood.

Then, 'twas before my time, the Roman
 At yonder heaving hill would stare:
The blood that warms an English yeoman,
 The thoughts that hurt him, they were there.

There, like the wind through woods in riot,
 Through him the gale of life blew high;
The tree of man was never quiet:
 Then 'twas the Roman, now 'tis I.

The gale, it plies the saplings double,
 It blows so hard, 'twill soon be gone:
To-day the Roman and his trouble
 Are ashes under Uricon.

A.E.Housman (1859-1936)

Mitchell's Fold, Stapeley Hill

This stone circle sheathed Excalibur,
held back trickery, greed,
mischief, famine -
caught the witch who milked
the magic cow into a sieve.

These petrifying stones,
shunted and plundered,
trap scraps of the sacred,
hold stories. We huddle
to sense what remains.

The lark strikes -
soaring on song past
the circling peregrine.
Shrug off history, myth, feel winter's
hard dry bite on over-grazed grass.

Bracken is slow to fiddle cattle
to this high summer pasture
shelved between countries
tipped between times where
paths and sightlines scramble;

traipsed by axe-traders,
farmers, miners, trippers.

Chris Kinsey

Tortoiseshells at Lydbury North

Church-shy, I'm drawn from shivering
amongst graves and the surplices of snowdrops
to the plain page of the south transept.

Curious, not for names on a register,
or details of the ceremony, just for
a sense of where my grandparents married.

Lattice light, candles and Christmas roses,
all blanched like vellum. I lift a latch
and discover stairs to the school-room.

Casual as confetti, small tortoiseshell wings
scatter oak steps. Scraps of torn manuscript -
one side charred and brown, the other

illuminated with summer: mimulus,
nasturtium, ink spots, borders
filled with lunules of speedwell.

I speculate on their fall:
kindled from hibernation by winter sun,
a wild, fast fluttering, flames spiralling upwards

beating against glass traps until starved and exhausted,
they dropped to a flicker, ticking like snow striking slate,
stopped in a papery, ashy hush.

Chris Kinsey

Clive Sahib

From childhood I desired fortune and fame to be forever mine,
I wanted class, status, prominence and the world to remember,
a significant man, 1st Baron Robert Clive; England's treasure.

An adolescent "good for nothing, a tearaway, a spoiled brat".
Young and feral like a Bengal tiger waiting to be let loose
out of a simple Shropshire village into the vast land of India.

I worked for the East India Company - like a prison sentence,
depression overtook me; I drank potions of hate and rage,
then joined the army. I rose rapidly and lucratively to the top.

From a clerk to a conqueror, the Empire belonged to me,
pride and victory for England, I focused on power and politics;
I showed them what I was all about. I was the British Raj.

I laughed at natives, their funny looking gods and goddesses,
I had power and position, born to a category of superior race,
seized with cannons, heartless strengths, a craze to snatch it all.

India was a goldmine; I wasn't letting it slip into any other hands,
I fought off the French, the Dutch or anyone who got in the way.
I bribed, looted, killed the Indians, the foolish, inferior natives.

Maharajas, lands, *sandhi*, treaties, *lagaan*, very easily bought.
I grabbed riches, took them back to Shropshire to live like a king;
my family and friends turned on me; my wealth was the problem.

I have everything, yet nothing at all; life isn't as splendid;
unsatisfied, broken, the end has come; opium, a knife, a gun.
I have been defeated by life; a memory of pride and greed.

Kuli Kohli

Maharajas - any of various Indian princes – rulers of the former native states.
Sandhi - a binding agreement / treaty (Punjabi). Lagaan – taxes (Hindi).

Christmas Eve Walk to the Burrow in Deep Snow

This winter night is lighter out. I'm heavy
with custom, candle fat, goose grease.
Stove smoke steaming the windows blind. I leave
my children, tinsel, the cloying sweetmeats.

Ten steps out, it's like swimming,
my trace erased in the trick of the white
that's level to a pheasant's eye. He and I
the only mistakes on this silent night.

Heaving his Christmas pudding body
above a holly hedge, startled, barely flight,
he lumbers straight into a fence.
His scaly ankle's ensnared, his fear tight.

I close his crazing wings, stroke his petrol
throat. Under the feathered illusion of fat,
just bone. I unwind him from the wire,
he stutters home. There's only love in this act.

The ditches of the fort are full of drifts;
the vertical drama of ramparts doused.
All the temperamental ground's tempered,
its misshapes and history un-roused.

There could be fish beneath me
frozen in their ponds. I could be walking
on a grave, a horde, an abandoned baby.
I'd never know. The snow unlearns everything.

The black hawthorn edges
mapping out the moonlit white
are not the only guide for home.
The way will not grow dark tonight.

Janie Mitchell

*The Burrow is an Iron Age hill fort above Hopesay which I walked to
from one side as a child and the other as an adult.*

Ex Soldier on the street in Telford

He stares ahead while others beg for coins,
enough to score clean needles and a fix
that guarantee a brief oblivion
from doorway piss and sodden cardboard dens,
a limbo world of hidden damaged lives
of silence within layers of loneliness.
Sometimes the past and present interweave.
A falling coin becomes a cartridge case
ejected from a burnt out blackened breech
of cold gun metal pressed against his throat.
The hidden trip wired mines and burning tanks
flame into fear that still flares deep inside.
It's then he wakes and struggles to recall
brief fragments of a past identity,
like faint graffiti on a barracks wall.
By these leaking bivouacs some share with dogs
each territory is staked out, fiercely fought
as evolution snarls and culls at night
when shifting pecking orders on the street
ensure only the fittest will survive.

Don Nixon

A politician visits a local care home

Is this the year that you'll become a Knight
as tirelessly you run the Honours race?
We hide a smile but we all know our place,
as you perform this pre-election rite.
Your boarding school tight vowels and high voice
project crisp diphthongs dormitory shrill,
the timbre like an orthopaedic drill,
as you fire questions, giving little choice
to inmates you so graciously select.
No thorny problem is for you too dense,
or way beyond your self-styled commonsense
to solve, while never pausing to reflect.
For photographs you hold a patient's tray,
another step to that elusive K.

Don Nixon

The history of goose

She can trace hers back to Milburga's flock –
her ancestry – like Russian dolls, a bird in a bird
in a bird. Migration of angel-down and broken shell.
Out of the nibbled barley folds of Stoke St Milborough,
inheritance forthcoming in each quill. Each beakful of corn,
a hiss and a prayer. Breathless embryos within an egg
within an egg within an egg, their wry-necks furled
around their legs. Their soft yellow feet treading
a skein of albumen, between earth and heaven.

Miriam Obrey

From **Uriconium, An Ode**

For here lie remnants from a banquet table –
Oysters and marrow-bones, and seeds of grape –
The statement of whose age must sound a fable;
And Samian jars, whose sheen and flawless shape
      Look fresh from potter's mould.
Plasters with Roman finger-marks impressed;
Bracelets, that from the warm Italian arm
      Might seem to be scarce cold;
And spears – the same that pushed the Cymry west –
Unblunted yet; with tools of forge and farm
Abandoned, as a man in sudden fear
Drops what he holds to help his swift career:
For sudden was Rome's flight, and wild the alarm.
The Saxon shock was like Vesuvius' qualm.

Wilfred Owen

Roundel

In Shrewsbury Town e'en Hercules wox tired,
Tired of the streets that end not up nor down;
Tired of the Quarry, though seats may be hired
                Of Shrewsbury Town.

Tired of the tongues that knew not his renown;
Tired of the Quarry Bye-Laws, so admired
By the Salopian, the somnambulant clown.

Weak as a babe, and in like wise attired,
He leaned upon his club; frowned a last frown,
And of ineffable boredom, so expired
                In Shrewsbury Town.

Wilfred Owen (1893-1918)

Brown Clee Intruder

This evening I walk a forest trail,
come upon an unexpected pond,
its surface still as dusted gel.
I kneel at the edge, look across.
Water fleas skate the water's skin
as if pulled by invisible threads,
each their own insect coracle;
in tall, red tipped grass stalks
stubbling the soupy shallows
emerald damselflies dip and rise
going about egg related tasks
in horizontal, stuck-together pairs;
and higher up, above everything,
bright plasticine faced dragonflies
patrol on circuits of surveillance,
purposefully clipping one another
in patches of overlapping air space.

July muscle-heat stretches out,
crew cut sheep keep a distance
in the rough surrounding woods.
I sense my trespass, leave.

Nick Pearson

Under Titterstone Radar

RIP Mitch –
his name is everywhere,
white-stencilled inside old sheds,
daubed on sheer rocks
at the pool.

They raced old cars,
gunned and hand-braked them
to nervous wrecks,
then left them
out on the mud to die.

There is a body
in the deep, cold water.
When it is clear
you can see black tyres,
a side door opening skywards.

Aliens come here
at night,
they hum down,
their blue lights circling
against the crater's floor.

The white golf ball
guides them in,
beckons them from the east
to watch over
those who remember.

Nick Pearson

Wenlock Edge

At night, when you were homesick,
your brother told you to look up
and think of us at home,
continents away, watching the same
shared moon.

This field closens us, too.
When you come back I'll show you
how it tilts up to The Edge,
how wind, soughing through bands of ash and hazel,
marks that boundary, like falling into space.
Today, a sky lark hangs, rising and rising.
Its fluttering song fills the basin of the air.

Ice once clunked and ground its way here,
sliced through hills, thawed to a broth.
Now every stone turned over at the field edge
carries the memory of warm seas:
coral, stone lily and shattered ammonite.
The earth ploughs itself endlessly,
churns up its treasures.
It settles and moves,
understands no boundaries, secretly
brings us together.

Jeff Phelps

After the Deluge

Ducks are in the birdhouse
where the robin used to sit.
They're eating from the bread bin
which is floating next to it.

Eels are in the meter cupboard
getting electric shocks.
Water voles are reproducing
in the letter box.

There's a heron in the kitchen
where the blender used to be
and he's dipping in the fridge for
frozen kippers for his tea.

Rice grows in the rockery,
the drive is full of trout,
and even plastic gnomes are pulling
seven pounders out.

You have to see the funny side
and have a little grin –
with all our downstairs upstairs
and all the outside in,

I never really knew that
there was so much life out there;
but now I watch it floating past
from the comfort of my chair.

Jeff Phelps

Mortimer Forest

All afternoon the drone of a saw has fanned
with resin over this bank of vibrating pines;
with each completed sever, falling an octave –
the one, only, sound of another human
in all dead, hot, black, Mortimer Forest.

I have seen the place; clearing, sawdust, tarpaulin,
pipe-bottle, that is all, never the man.

If it stops now and I go there I will find,
to mark hard work for so long, long weeping ranks,
curtailed, seasoning in glutinous tiers,
and dust, dust red wood-ants perpetually sift.

Peter Reading

Burning Stubble

All stubble is being burned, a chiffon pall
is settling over round flesh-tint hills, it seems haunches
of supine bodies unbreathing after a fall.

We see them for the last time, all those men, their huge
efficient harvest; last light is pressing the panes.

Off the Teme at this season fog sinks us all, snuffs each
light in the low water-meadow out.

        We have grown
to expect these things here at this time (late harvest),
pyres, the extinguishing suck of mists
on September dusks, as we expect
winter thrushes in season and
the dark swift coming and going.

Peter Reading (1946-2011)

Boondocks

A friend once wrote to me from the 'Boondocks'
saying how I'd love it there, in that part of the USA
with "places called 'Dry Fork Creek,' 'Pleasant View,'
'Ashland City,' (which, he said, was the size of Netherton,
the village where I was born), and best of all 'Toadsuck'."

Imagine these on a dusty highway,
two shack backdroughts (for there is no water).
Cars red rusty in the front yard, rocking chair,
pick-up truck, fridge on the porch.

I sent back a letter saying I'd been exploring closer to home
clombering the lunar pincushion of the Stiperstones; peering
out across the plain for sign of the invaders who would wake Edric,
waiting for his warlord rumble beneath me; sitting on the Devil's Chair,
bristling, in an expectation that I'd deny, pooh-pooh,
laugh at from behind the shield of my sophistication.

The Dogger, Fisher, German Bight of poetic overuse, of melancholy
moodiness, might sing a knitting of a weathered identity for an island race

but we're all victim of the mould of our names
long before they become the self-expression of our signatures
when all we can do is claim them back with embellishment,
conjure with the resonance of Shelve and Snailbeach,
Plox Green and Bridges, the shuffle of Gravels, the suck of The Bog,

and remember a folding tin table, whose legs creaked as erected,
with the kingdoms of England: Wessex; Essex; Mercia; Northumbria,
adorned, that carried the Thermos soul of our picnics in Carding Mill
Valley where the day-out child booted a ball,
ran up and rolled down such impossible heights
and cooled off summer feet in a song that tumbled from the hills.

Dave Wm Reeves

The English Bridge, Shrewsbury

The spring was late this year.
Decades seemed to pass
In the bleak months
Since the last leaves dried
And fell, to shred and crumble
In the shroud grey days,
While birds hunched, hooded,
In the charcoal trees.

We were impatient
For the watercolour gold of willows,
Wet on wet reflection
In the green shine
Of a slow river.

Spring was late this year,
The dark nights
Long, cold tunnels in the mind.
We were bone weary of the wait
For sun and celandines
And early morning birdsong,
For the softness of the light.

Iris Rhodes

Cygnets on the Severn

And here they are, now grown
And stronger than we saw them months ago,
Struggling on the springtime flood
As currents sucked and swirled
And frantic parents fought against the flow.

Now calm, serene and slow,
Pearled water rolling silver from their heads,
They navigate through fallen yellow leaves,
Circled with light – and safe –
Parting the sheltering trails,
The golden curves of willows.

Iris Rhodes

At David Austin's

Bedded with A Shropshire Lad and Lass,
Wild Edric, velvety and pink,

draws oos and ahs from parties
of linen skirts and Panamas

who come here to revel in
this most midsummery of sights.

As hands reach to grasp green stems,
bringing noses nearer to the scent,

(which some describe as cucumber and cloves
where others find a hint of watercress),

collective gasps are heard. Wild Edric –
at home in David Austin's tea-rooms

lording it over rose-patterned plates
of dainty cakes and scones – is still at heart

a border rebel. Those velvet petals
hide a shieldwall of fine thorns.

Jane Seabourne

In January, 1917

More than standing on Haughmond Hill,
breathing in good Shropshire air,
he wanted dry feet: he needed new socks.

More than his Bond Street uniform,
he needed razor blades.

More than his volume of Keats,
he needed a celluloid hair-pin box from Boots.
It must have a tight-fitting lid;

more than all the Odes, more than Bright Star,
more than Hyperion, more than Lamia,
it should contain boracic powder.

More than a night in Lime House,
he needed Player's 'Navy Cut'.

More than the words to capture
this universal pervasion of ugliness,
he needed ink pellets.

He needed sweets so much,
he gave them exclamation marks,
as if to point out how strange that was.

More than all the above,
he wrote home from the mud, rain and frost,
to tell his mother he needed socks.

Not old. Not darned. Not shrunk.
He wanted dry feet. He needed new socks.

Jane Seabourne

The Little Hill

This is the hill, ringed by the misty shire –
The mossy, southern hill,
The little hill where larches climb so high.
Among the stars aslant
They chant;
Along the purple lower slopes they lie
In lazy golden smoke, more faint, more still
Than the pale woodsmoke of the cottage fire.
Here some calm Presence takes me by the hand
And all my heart is lifted by the chant
Of them that lean aslant
In golden smoke and sing, and softly bend:
And out from every larch-bole steals a friend.

Mary Webb

Hill Pastures

High on the hill the curlews and the whimbrels
Go mating all day long with a sweet whistle;
With a sound chiming bells and shaken timbrels,
And silver rings that fall in a crystal cup.
They laugh, as lovers laugh when the moon is up,
Over the cotton-grass and the carline thistle.

Poised in his airy spiral the snipe is calling,
Summoning love with a music mournful and lonely
As a lost lamb in the night, rising, falling,
Stranger than any melody, wilder than song.
He cries of life that is short, and death that is long,
Telling his dusky love to one heart only.

Once in seven days a plaintive ringing
Sounds from the little chapel high in the heather,
Out with the sorrowful snipe and the whimbrel winging.
The wild hill ponies hear it there as they graze,
And whinny, and call to their foals, and stand at gaze,
Hearing a clear voice in the clear weather.

And out of pine-dark farms and windy places,
And quiet cottages low in the valley hiding,
Brown folk come with still and wistful faces.
Straying by twos and threes, like the peaceful sheep,
Into the small brown shippen of souls they creep,
Seeking a calm like the hills', but more abiding.

Mary Webb (1881-1927)

Grey Serendipity

like a mountain.
What luck to come by a coat
the colour of frost shadows
with nothing in the pockets
but a few cold coins of archaeology,
says the man with stick arms
protruding from rolled up shirt sleeves.
My mind is not much use to me
while I'm thinking;
I can't help repeating the past, he says,
'cause I'm conditioned. That's how I've
been taught to think. All my experiences are
old through recognition.
Under the burden of generations, a laden branch
yo-yoing in and out of history, he asks:
Would it be sanity to deny the false
while not knowing the truth?
stick arms protruding like – well; like
stick arms protruding from rolled up shirt sleeves.
Would you believe?
They've built cathedrals of ice
from frozen thoughts
to be comfortable in.
An Anglo/Welsh eye
counts stars over Bryn Offa.
I'll build a memorial to it out of molehills,
tattoo my arms with Cox's Orange Pippins,
and sign an affidavit disclaiming knowledge.
Those who say they know are lying.
From a stone book opened at 'Worthy Causes',
he reads an inventory of names.
No-No-No, he says to thunderous advice.
Today I'll make a gift of 'clouded vision'
for the respectable to perform
endoscopic miracles on the NHS

W. Geof Williams

day trippers to pant

come from the town to see how it is;
look down there i say, as guide to a busload,
and they peer down the kilns, see abortions,
smell the burnt out dreams, the buried beliefs decomposing -
no longer needed, i say - except when the locals want to escape
from a fact into unreality -
after all who needs a belief that there's a rattling wind,
sunshine and that sometimes life is tough?
yeah there's something cruel in this rock face; see those bleached
bones and the buzzard over the bottomless quarry pool where
'happy tom' of the apposite name became a drowned celebrity
overnight.
duw - i say,
there's dancin' pugh in his blue suede boots,
no bigger than the sharp end of nothing
and jinny wet-leg from the school house,
needing more than any man can give - both adding a bit of colour.
- come over here! I shout - meet emrys 'kid' jones - king of the welsh
lightweights in the fifties - see how he hangs onto the day moving
through title fights etched in blood on the roped in canvas of his brain
- face like the back wall of a cave
- at his best fighting the English - for the price of a pint
- sits down every time he hears a bell - and that's most of the time.
we stop at the 'gyn wheel' why so called, somebody asks,
but i can't tell them, and the gentle hum of wheeled laughter
rewinds the round remembered moments.
reconstituting the past - is it?
well - maybe - look at us;
emrys still living the dream - while we
grovel in the ground ashes and dust
of the mind's broken images.
bit frightening
- innit?

W. Geof Williams

Crossing the Rhuddwr

Often we cross that streamlet into another country;
The only sign of our alienation –
The signs.

There was a time when crossing was momentous;
A bloody line drawn in clear water;
A castle to oversee the passage:

Bryn Amlwg – a hill with a view.
Now it is an archaeologist's figment,
The keep unkempt into peaceful walls:

That farmhouse, these barns;
Leaving only a grassy knoll,
A cropped footnote to history.

It was garrisoned in times of trouble
With men who had learned
To shout: 'Bugger off,' in Welsh

To marauders from Ceri
With a *hiraeth* for free English sheep;
Hanging one or two for emphasis.

Some Fridays we pillage Newtown markets for Welsh lamb,
Pay in notes that lack their Prince's aged head
And return across the water unchallenged.

*   *   *   *   *

In a boundary suit of 1567:
'Witness remembered double hanging 60 years before.
One man was hanged by Clun officers while simultaneously,
across the brook less than a bowshot away, the officers of
Kerry dispatched the other.'

Trans. Shrops, Arch. Soc. 1888 p.258

Alan Wilson

59

The Goat on the Roof*

The goats that graze round Craven Arms
Bleat together ragged psalms,
The burden of this hircine choir
Celebrates a green messiah.
This visionary used to roam
Around the Centre's grassy dome,
Preaching of climate's downward climb
To passers on the Fortynine.
'Cut your mileage, plant a tree,
Eat no meat and keep a bee.
Cease to wash be aromatic,
Grow a beard and get ecstatic.
The end is nigh so sound a horn;
Let's hear it for Capricorn.'
This eschatologic hope –
Terminated – too much rope.

Alan Wilson

*The Secret Hills Discovery Centre has a turf roof.
  On this, grown shaggy, a 'mower' was tethered.

Acknowledgements

Hopton Castle is from Vuyelwa Carlin's *how we dream of the dead*, Seren, 1995, used with permission.

The *Peat-Cutters* from the sequence *Kingdom of Sphagnum* and *The Women of Whixall* in *The Echoing Green*, Flambard, 2001, reprinted by permission of Gladys Mary Coles.

Fred D'Aguiar's poem *I Walk around Ellesmere* was written while poet-in-residence at Mythstories, Wem, in 2004. www.mythstories.com

Catherine Fisher's poem *Archivist*, reproduced by permission of Pollinger Limited and Catherine Fisher, also came out of a Mythstories residency, 2005. It refers to Richard Gough's *History of Myddle*, written in 1700.

Local History by Simon Fletcher appeared in the *Tettenhall Record* and *Cannon's Mouth*. *Loot* was published in *Dreamcatcher, Email from the Provinces*, Pennine Pens, 2000, and *Another Bridge*, Sahitya Press, 2012.

Paul Francis's *Langley Chapel* appeared in the *Wenlock Poetry Festival Anthology*, 2012 and *Odd Couple* was previously published in *Olympians*, Bridgnorth Writers' Group, 2012.

Roger Garfitt's *Border Songs* were engraved on glass screens in the County Records & Research Centre, Shrewsbury, and published in *Selected Poems*, Carcanet, 2000. All the quotations are taken from Arthur Raistrick's history of the Coalbrookdale Company, *Dynasty of Iron Founders*.

Marilyn Gunn's poems are from *Words from the Glasshouse*, Liberty Books, 2013.

Frances Horovitz poem from *Selected Poems*, Bloodaxe, 1989, used with permission.

A.E.Housman poems from *A Shropshire Lad*.

Chris Kinsey's *Tortoiseshells at Lydbury North* appeared in her collection *Swarf* from Smokestack Books, 2011.

Wilfred Owen's *Uriconium* extract and *Roundel* from *The Poems of Wilfred Owen*, Edited by Jon Stallworthy, Chatto & Windus, 1983. Used with permission.

Jeff Phelps's *After the Deluge* appeared in *Reading Allowed*, Bridgnorth Writers' group.

Peter Reading's poems from *Collected Poems 1, Poems 1970-1984*, Bloodaxe Books, 1995, used with permission.

Mary Webb's poems *Hill Pastures* and *The Little Hill* from *Selected Poems of Mary Webb*, ed. Gladys Mary Coles, Headland, 2005.

Brief Biographies

Jean Atkin works as a writer and educator and lives in Shropshire. She is a past winner of the Torbay Prize, the Ravenglass Poetry Prize and others. Her first collection *Not Lost Since Last Time* was published by Oversteps Books, 2013.

Mollie Bolt is originally from Hertfordshire but moved to Shropshire 36 years ago and began to write poetry soon afterwards, drawing inspiration from music, an acute sense of place and many years as a military wife.

Rosamund Brown completed an MA in Creative Writing in 2010, producing a poetry collection about Shropshire. This led to her membership of Shrewsbury Museum Writers' group and her work featuring in its 2012 exhibition. Published in several magazines.

David Calcutt is a poet and playwright and lives in Walsall. His most recent publication is *Road Kill*, a poetry collection written with Nadia Kingsley and published by Fair Acre Press. He is currently working on a new one-man play.

Vuyelwa Carlin has had four collections of poetry published by Seren Books. She grew up in East Africa but has lived in the Shropshire countryside for the last forty years, a landscape she says that 'has sunk into my soul'.

Keith Chandler moved to Bridgnorth from Norfolk three years ago. His poetry has been published in four collections by Carcanet, OUP, Redbeck and Peterloo. www.KeithChandlerPoet.com

Marion Cockin was born in Wednesbury in the Black Country. She has had poetry published in *We're all in this together*, Offa's Press, 2012, and various national and regional magazines. She has been an Offa's Press partner since its beginnings in 2010.

Gladys Mary Coles is a multi-award winning poet with ten collections. Editor of fifteen anthologies. Her novel *Clay*, 2010, was long-listed for Wales Book of the Year. Biographer and authority on Mary Webb, President of Mary Webb Society. Runs Headland Press.

Janet Collins is a retired drama teacher and author of four children's novels (Blackie) set in the Shropshire countryside, one of which won the Kathleen Fidler Award. Enjoys spinning and weaving. Currently a volunteer in the Ironbridge Gorge Museum Archives.

Fred D'Aguiar was born in London, 1960, to Guyanese parents. His poetry collections include *Mama Dot, Bill of Rights, Bloodlines* and *Continental Shelf.* Since 2003 he's been Professor of English at Virginia Tech, USA. Twice short-listed for the TS Eliot Prize.

Cherry Doyle was born and raised in Shrewsbury and currently lives in Wolverhampton. She works full time and writes on the side including attending Blakenhall Writers' group.

Susan Fearn is a widely published poet whose work has appeared in numerous magazine and anthologies. She has worked with film makers and 3D artists.

Catherine Fisher is a poet and author of children's fiction. Awards include The Cardiff International Poetry Prize. *The Oracle* was shortlisted for the Whitbread Children's Book Prize. *Incarceron* was *The Times* Children's Book of the Year and *New York Times* Bestseller.

Simon Fletcher is a poet, workshop leader, tutor for the WEA and freelance writer. He's had three poetry collections published by Pennine Pens. His e-novel *Nanny Knows Best* is available on Kindle. He also performs with the multi-cultural Mini Mushaira. www.simonfletcher.net

Paul Francis, an active writer and performer, lives in Much Wenlock. He writes in a variety of styles, on a range of topics. His most recent collections are *Various Forms*, and *Boxed Set*, poems inspired by film and TV.

Roger Garfitt's *Border Songs* are engraved on glass screens in the County Archive in Shrewsbury. He performs *In All My Holy Mountain*, a celebration of Mary Webb, with the John Williams Septet to a score by the composer Nikki Iles. *Selected Poems* from Carcanet Press.

Marilyn Gunn spends a large part of her life on her allotment and in her greenhouse in Broseley. The poetry she writes there has become a life and a lifeline. *Words from the Glasshouse*, bringing together forty years of her poetry, was published in 2013.

Andrew Harrison (1947-2012) lived in Market Drayton and was known locally as an artist, writer, folk musician and conservationist. He took pleasure from the landscape of the Shropshire-Staffordshire border and this is reflected in much of his work.

Peter Holliday was born in the Welsh Marches and has lived in the area for more than 40 years. The landscape, history and folklore of Shropshire has always been important and often the subject of his poetry.

Frances Horovitz (1938-83) was greatly loved and respected not only as a poet, but also as a broadcaster and performer of poetry. She died, aged just 45, after a long illness. Her *Selected Poems* was published by Bloodaxe Books, 1989.

A E Housman (1859-1936) was a professor of Latin at Cambridge. Born in Worcestershire, *the blue remembered hills*, he noted, were those of an idealised Shropshire. His first book *A Shropshire Lad* was enormously popular with Tommies in the First World War.

Chris Kinsey has three collections of poetry: *Kung Fu Lullabies* and *Cure for a Crooked Smile* with Ragged Raven Press and *Swarf* with Smokestack Books. She also writes nature articles for *Cambria* and *Natur Cymru* and short dramas.

Kuli Kohli works for Wolverhampton City Council and is a member of the Blakenhall Writers' Group. She was born with mild cerebral palsy in India and moved to England at an early age. She lives in Wolverhampton with her family.

Janie Mitchell has had poetry anthologised by Virago and Flarestack and published in magazines. She is a singer-songwriter who's released 3 CDs, the latest being song settings of the poetry of Mary Webb.

Don Nixon has had poems and short stories published in UK and in North America. He won the formal poetry category at the Lake Orta International Poetry Festival, 2010 & 11 and the Leeds Peace Poetry prize. His novel *Ransom* was published this year.

Miriam Obrey has been published in *The North*, *The Rialto* and the *Oxford Poets Anthology*, 2007. A member of the Border Poets, Miriam is currently poet-in-residence at Westhope Craft College, Craven Arms.

Wilfred Owen (1893-1918) was born in Oswestry but his family lived in Shrewsbury at the time of his death in France. Greatly admired for his realistic poetry of warfare he has become acknowledged as one of the finest First World War poets.

Nick Pearson is a Shropshire based writer and poet who regularly reads at festivals and live literature events throughout the Midlands. *Made in Captivity* was published by Offa's Press in 2011.

Jeff Phelps's poems are widely published. *River Passage* is produced as a CD by Offa's Press with piano music by Dan Phelps. His novels, *Painter Man* and *Box of Tricks*, are published by Tindal Street Press. Jeff lives in Bridgnorth. www.jeffphelps.co.uk

Peter Reading (1946-2011) was born in Liverpool and studied painting at Liverpool College of Art. He lived for 40 years in Shropshire. He is the only British poet to have won the Lannan Award for Poetry twice.

Dave Reeves edited and published *Raw Edge Magazine*, for 13 years until 2009. He presents *re.Lit* the monthly live literature show for RadioWildfire.com and is poet-in-residence to the Black Country Living Museum. *Black Country Dialectics* was published by Offa's Press in 2011.

Iris Rhodes is a former teacher/ advisor for drama in education, her writing inspired by everything from Greek myths to bus shelters. She has been published in several anthologies and magazines and enjoys performing her work. She lives in South Staffs.

Jane Seabourne's debut collection, *Bright Morning*, was published by Offa's Press in 2010. In 2012, she co-edited *We're All in This Together*, an anthology of environmental poetry. Jane is a member of ImageTextImage, a collective of artists and writers.

Mary Webb (1881-1927). Six Shropshire novels including *Precious Bane* (winner, Prix Femina 1924-5) and *Gone to Earth*, 1917, a Novel of the Year and Hollywood film, 1948. Though primarily a poet, no collection was published in her lifetime. Her fame was posthumous.

Geof Williams is Welsh by birth, a former teacher, farmer, RAF PT instructor, artist, lorry driver and market stall holder. He is optimistic about the future but notes from the natural world an easy transition to the inner landscape of confusion and anxiety.

Alan Wilson is a gentleman of leisure come on hard times. Resident on the border for 20 years. Was Bettws PCC secretary. Is the parish hall secretary. Writes poetry while waiting for remission.